Contents

Contents

Preface

Negotiation is a fundamental personal skill that can be learned. The skill of negotiation is used by people engaged in business or community activities, but often overlooked by the same people in the conduct of their daily lives. Everyone needs to know how to negotiate. For those who are fearful of the process, or too embarrassed to try, this book can help.

Successful Negotiation presents concepts that can be applied in any situation where negotiation is the method by which issues are resolved. Those who master the skill of effective negotiation will save money, save time and achieve a high degree of need satisfaction. Skilled negotiators don't have to worry about 'what might have been'.

Successful Negotiation has a unique self-paced format that encourages the reader to become personally involved. Designed to be 'read with a pencil', there are abundant exercises, activities, assessments and cases that invite participation.

This book can be used effectively in a number of ways. Here are some possibilities:

● Individual study. Because the book is self-instructional, all that is needed is a quiet place, some time and a pencil. Completing the activities and exercises will provide valuable feedback, as well as practical ideas for self-improvement.

● Workshops and seminars. This book is ideal for use during, or as pre-assigned reading prior to a workshop or seminar. With the basics in hand, the quality of participation will improve. More time can be spent practising concept extensions and applications during the programme.

● College programmes. Thanks to the format, brevity and low cost, this book is ideal for short courses and extension programmes.

There are other possibilities that depend on the objectives of the user. One thing is for sure, even after it has been read, this book will serve as an excellent reference tool which can be easily reviewed.

Robert B Maddux

To the Reader

In approximately one hour you will have learned enough about the fundamentals of negotiating from this book to repay the purchase price several times over.

You will be encouraged to complete a number of exercises that provide an opportunity to apply the concepts which are presented. You will also have a chance to do some self-analysis in order to identify your negotiating strengths and weaknesses.

What you learn, and how effectively you are able to apply it, depend on how carefully you read, *and* how thoughtfully you practise and apply the principles presented.

CHAPTER 1
Your Objectives

Before you begin this book, give some thought to your objectives.

Objectives give us a sense of direction, a definition of what we plan to accomplish, and a feeling of fulfilment when they are achieved.

Tick the objectives below that are important to you. Then when you have completed the book, review your objectives and enjoy the sense of achievement you will feel.

Which objectives do you want to achieve?

Once I have completed this book, I hope to:

identify opportunities for negotiation more readily. ☐

understand the importance of deciding what I need, as compared with what I want. ☐

recognise why thorough preparation *prior* to beginning a negotiation is essential. ☐

remember the sequential nature of negotiation and why each step is important. ☐

be able to employ a variety of negotiation strategies and tactics which will meet my needs. ☐

enter confidently into a negotiation with a win/win philosophy. ☐

CHAPTER 2
What is Negotiation?

You are about to embark on a brief study of the principles of negotiation. You already have an interest or you wouldn't be reading this book. You probably want to learn more about negotiation or how to become more proficient as a negotiator. Let's start by comparing some of your ideas with those of the author.

Your ideas

1. In the space below, write what the word 'negotiation' means to you.

   _____

   _____

   _____

   _____

2. What prompts negotiation between companies, groups and/or individuals?

   _____

   _____

   _____

   _____

3. How frequently do most people negotiate?
   Very rarely ☐
   Almost every day ☐
   A few times each year ☐

Now compare your thoughts with those of the author.

Most people think goods have a fixed price and that it would be inappropriate to suggest bargaining to reduce it. Yet three-quarters of the world's population buy and sell merchandise without a fixed price. The value of goods is determined through negotiation between buyer and seller.

Price is not the only variable in negotiation. Other considerations include: interest rate, delivery date, size, quality, quantity, colour, warranty and service.

Any aspect of a transaction that is not totally satisfactory to you is worth negotiating.

CHAPTER 3
Negotiation – Some Practical Definitions

The following are some accepted definitions of negotiation:

1. Whenever we attempt to influence another person through an exchange of ideas, or something of material value, we are negotiating. *Negotiation is the process we use to satisfy our needs when someone else controls what we want.* Every wish we would like to fulfil, every need we feel compelled to satisfy, is a potential situation for negotiation. Other terms are often applied to this process, such as bargaining, haggling, mediating or bartering.

2. Negotiation between companies, groups or individuals normally occurs *because one has something the other wants and is willing to bargain to get it.*

3. Most of us are constantly involved in negotiations to one degree or another. Examples include: when people meet to draw up contracts; buy or sell anything; resolve differences; make mutual decisions; or agree on work plans. Even deciding where to have lunch makes use of the negotiating process.

Danger

There is a danger of being in the midst of negotiation without recognising it. If this occurs, you will not be able to try to improve the outcome for yourself. If you have not thought of the transaction as a negotiation, and have not prepared, the chances are the results will be less favourable for you than they might have been.

CHAPTER 4

Identifying Opportunities for Negotiation

Many people miss the opportunity to make a more favourable exchange because they fail to recognise the opportunity to negotiate. Are you missing opportunities? Test yourself.

Here is a list of typical transactions. Tick those that offer an opportunity to improve your position through negotiation.

1. Purchasing an appliance at a department store. ☐
2. Deciding with the family which film to see. ☐
3. Getting a pay rise. ☐
4. Selecting a contractor to build a new home. ☐
5. Working out an effective date for an employee transfer. ☐
6. Deciding on a date for the next meeting of your study group. ☐
7. Agreeing on realistic deadlines. ☐
8. Buying plants for your new rose garden. ☐
9. Deciding who has the use of the car for the weekend. ☐
10. Agreeing on a change of work rules with the union. ☐

List below other negotiating situations in which are you apt to find yourself.

_____

_____

_____

_____

Are you prepared to handle them effectively?

_____

Answer

Give yourself a perfect score if you ticked all 10 items. Everything is negotiable! Whether you pursue that reality or not is strictly up to you. It does on occasion require some courage and effort. You have to know what you want to achieve, and what you are willing to settle for. You must also know what you are willing to give up to get what you want.

CHAPTER 5
Disagreement and Conflict

Successful negotiators have a positive attitude. They are able to view conflict as normal and constructive. The skills they use to resolve conflict are not magic, they can be learned. These skills, once learned, provide the courage and confidence necessary to challenge others, and initiate a positive negotiation. Understanding the skills of negotiation also sustains us when we are challenged by others.

Overleaf are several statements about personal reactions to disagreement and conflict. Circle the number that best describes you. The higher the number, the more you agree with the statement. When you finish, total the numbers you circled and write the figure in the space provided.

	Strong agreement					*Mild agreement*				
It doesn't bother me to question a price or seek a more favourable exchange than offered.	10	9	8	7	6	5	4	3	2	1
I have nothing to lose in seeking a better deal if I do it in a reasonable way.	10	9	8	7	6	5	4	3	2	1
Conflict is a fact of life and I work hard to resolve it.	10	9	8	7	6	5	4	3	2	1
Conflict is positive because it makes me examine my ideas carefully.	10	9	8	7	6	5	4	3	2	1
In resolving conflict, I try to consider the needs of the other person.	10	9	8	7	6	5	4	3	2	1
Conflict often produces better solutions to problems.	10	9	8	7	6	5	4	3	2	1
Conflict stimulates my thinking and sharpens my judgement.	10	9	8	7	6	5	4	3	2	1
Working with conflict has taught me that compromise is not a sign of weakness.	10	9	8	7	6	5	4	3	2	1
Satisfactorily resolved, conflict often strengthens relationships.	10	9	8	7	6	5	4	3	2	1
Conflict is a way to test one's own point of view.	10	9	8	7	6	5	4	3	2	1

TOTAL_____

If you scored 80 or above you have a realistic attitude towards conflict, and seem willing to work to resolve it. If you scored between 50 and 79 you appear to be dealing fairly well with conflict, but need to work towards a more positive approach.

If your score was below 50, you need first to understand why, and then work hard to learn techniques of conflict resolution. By the time you finish this book, you may wish to complete this exercise again.

CHAPTER 6
Develop a Win/Win Philosophy

The importance of attitude in negotiating

Our attitude is always important, and this is especially true in negotiating. Attitudes influence our objectives, and objectives control the way we negotiate. The way in which we negotiate determines the outcome.

Have you thought about your objectives when you negotiate? Have you considered those of the other party? Can you both win?

Each party in a negotiation wants to win. Successful negotiations end with something both need. Any time a negotiator approaches a bargaining situation with the idea, 'I must win, and really don't care about the other party' disaster is close at hand.

The win/win concept of negotiation is not simply based on ethical considerations. When both parties to an agreement are satisfied with the outcome, they will work to make it succeed, not fail. They will also be willing to work with one another in the future. Perhaps you are asking, 'How can I come out ahead in a negotiation, if I permit the other party to meet their needs as well?' The answer to this question lies in the fact that different people have different needs. How many people have exactly the same needs as you? Win/win negotiating is simply good business. The person who ends a negotiation feeling that he or she has been had, may try to get even later.

Think for a minute, and then check your reasoning with that of the author.

Win/Win negotiating is possible because...

Individuals, groups, organisations or nations entering negotiation with each other all have reasons to negotiate. Since these reasons are unique to the parties involved, and because each party will place different values on their wants and needs, an exchange is usually possible where each party can obtain what is of greatest value to them at that time.

In successful negotiation, a negotiator will obtain something of greater value in exchange for something on which he or she places a lower relative value. Both parties can win. They may have wished for more, but end up satisfied.

Benjamin Franklin expressed it best when he said, 'Trades would not take place unless it were advantageous to the parties concerned. Of course, it is better to strike as good a bargain as one's bargaining position admits. The worst outcome is when by overriding greed, no bargain is struck, and a trade that could have been advantageous to both parties, does not come off at all.'

Win/Win negotiating has some distinct characteristics. In the list below, tick those you already possess.

1. I have a win/win attitude. ☐
2. I understand and can apply the basic techniques of conflict resolution. ☐
3. I am genuinely interested in the needs of the other party. ☐
4. I am flexible in my approach and willing to make some concessions to get what I want. ☐
5. I am cooperative. ☐

6. I understand the importance of the give/get principle in negotiating. ☐

7. I am willing to think through the objective of the negotiation in terms of my wants, actual needs and the values involved in advance. ☐

8. I have the patience to educate the other person as to the logic of my position rather than trying to bluster my way through. ☐

CHAPTER 7

The Give/Get Principle of Negotiating

For some, the word compromise has a negative meaning. For others, it describes the necessary give and take of everyday living. It is normally not possible to get something for nothing – there always seems to be a cost or concession that must be made to receive what you want. The word compromise simply means making and/or receiving concessions.

See how the principle works on page 18.

BASIC APPROACHES TO NEGOTIATION

PARTY A	PARTY B

FORMULA 1

Give/Get   Give/Get

Both parties are willing to give something in order to get what they want and enter the negotiation with that in mind. How much, and when they compromise are the details to be worked out. This formula has the most potential for success.

FORMULA 2

Give/Get   Get/Give

Formula 2 also has a good chance of success because both sides understand that a good settlement requires both giving and getting. One party is willing to give provided something comes back in return. The other party will give after having received. The difficulty in this formula is that the getter may decide to see how much can be got without giving in return. If the getter goes too far, or waits too long to reciprocate, the giver may decide to revoke concessions previously made and the parties may reach a stalemate.

FORMULA 3

Get/Give   Get/Give

In this formula, both parties come into a negotiation with the idea they will give nothing until they receive. They will stalemate quickly and remain there unless one party is willing to risk giving in order to get. If neither party budges, there is no negotiation.

CHAPTER 8
Characteristics of a Successful Negotiator

So far you have had a chance to compare your negotiating concepts with those of the author. Now would be a good time to evaluate your personal characteristics as a negotiator. Some people do not become good negotiators until they rethink their approach.

This scale is based on personal characteristics necessary to successful negotiation. It can help you to decide the potential you already possess and also identify areas where improvement is needed. Circle the number that best reflects where you fall on the scale. The higher the number the more the characteristic describes you. When you have finished, total the numbers circled in the space provided.

I am sensitive to the needs of others.	10 9 8 7 6 5 4 3 2 1
I will compromise to solve problems when necessary.	10 9 8 7 6 5 4 3 2 1
I am committed to a win/win philosophy.	10 9 8 7 6 5 4 3 2 1
I have a high tolerance for conflict.	10 9 8 7 6 5 4 3 2 1
I am willing to research and analyse issues fully.	10 9 8 7 6 5 4 3 2 1
Patience is one of my strong points.	10 9 8 7 6 5 4 3 2 1
My tolerance for stress is high.	10 9 8 7 6 5 4 3 2 1
I am a good listener.	10 9 8 7 6 5 4 3 2 1
Personal attack and ridicule do not bother me unduly.	10 9 8 7 6 5 4 3 2 1
I can identify bottom line issues quickly.	10 9 8 7 6 5 4 3 2 1

TOTAL_____

If you scored 80 or above, you have characteristics of a good negotiator. You recognise what negotiating requires and seem willing to apply yourself accordingly. If you scored between 60 and 79, you should do well as a negotiator but have some characteristics that need further development.

If your evaluation is below 60, you should go over the items again carefully. You may have been hard on yourself, or you may have identified some key areas on which to concentrate as you negotiate. Repeat this evaluation after you finish this book, and again after you have had practice in negotiating.

CHAPTER 9
The Six Basic Steps in Negotiating

You are making good progress. It is now time to look at the six basic steps in the negotiating process. Each step, regardless of the time it takes, is required. For this reason many people think of negotiation as almost ritualistic. Once you understand the steps and their purpose you will be able to meet any negotiating challenge effectively.

Hazel, a woman in need of a new fridge/freezer will be our guide.

Step 1. Getting to know one another

Negotiating is like any social situation that has a business purpose. It moves more smoothly when the parties take a little time to get to know one another. It is helpful to assess those involved before negotiations begin. Individual backgrounds will provide an excellent guide to the level of importance placed on the issues, and the degree of expertise brought to bear on the subject. As the process starts, you should observe, listen, and learn. A good rule of thumb is to keep the beginning friendly and relaxed, yet businesslike.

Hazel is interested in buying a new fridge/freezer. She has studied ads in the newspapers and selected an appliance shop that seems to have good prices. She has done enough homework to know exactly what she wants (she even has pictures of the models in which she is most interested) and a good idea of what she should pay. On entering the store, she introduces herself to a salesperson, learns his name, and tells him she would like to have someone who knows about fridge/freezers to show her different models. She will observe the salesperson's attitude and approach to the sale closely to pick up clues as to the store's sales policies, willingness to bargain and desire to satisfy new customers.

Step 2. Statement of goals and objectives

After the opening, negotiating normally flows into a general statement of goals and objectives by the parties involved. Specific issues may not be raised at this time because each party is just beginning to explore the needs of the other. The person who speaks first on the issues may say, for example, 'I would like to ensure that this agreement works in a way that is beneficial to everyone concerned.' No terms have been suggested yet, but a positive statement has been made on behalf of an agreement being reached, which is favourable to all concerned.

The person making the opening statement should then wait for feedback from the other party to learn if they have similar goals or objectives. If there are differences, now is the time to learn them.

It is normally a good idea to make the initial statements positive and agreeable. This is no time for hostility or defensiveness. You need to build an atmosphere of cooperation and mutual trust.

As the salesperson offers to show Hazel the available fridge/freezers she comments: 'I hope I can find a model I like at a fair price. I was attracted to this store because you seem to be successful and to give the customer a good buy at the same time. I feel both are important.'

Step 3. Starting the process

Some negotiations are complex and have many issues to resolve. Others may only have a few. Also, individual issues may vary greatly in complexity. No one can predict the direction negotiations will take until both parties have presented the issues. There may be hidden needs neither party has raised, but these will surface as things proceed.

Often issues are bundled, so the solution to one is contingent on the solution to another. For example, 'I will not agree to buy the new furnace at that price unless a free one-year maintenance warranty is included.'

Conversely, there may be an attempt to separate issues to make them mutually exclusive. For example, in the sale of a furnished house, the seller may prefer to discuss the house and furnishings as separate negotiations. The buyer may feel they should be combined. In some negotiations, all issues are connected. No one issue is considered resolved until all have been resolved.

A skilled negotiator will study the issues closely *before* negotiations begin in order to determine where advantages lie with regard to splitting or combining issues.

Once the negotiators have reviewed the issues, they must begin dealing with them one by one. Opinions vary about whether to begin with a minor or major issue. Some feel negotiation should be started with a minor issue that has the potential of being easily resolved, because this will establish a favourable climate for additional agreements. Others feel that beginning with a major issue is best because unless it is satisfactorily resolved the others are unimportant.

> The salesperson responds to Hazel by asking what she wants in a fridge/freezer in terms of size, accessories and efficiency of operation. He also asks her for a price range. Hazel outlines her needs and the salesperson acknowledges they can be met by most of the manufacturers he represents. He does tell her, however, that she has selected some expensive options that will take her above her expressed price range. Hazel replies, 'I don't see why they should.'

Step 4. Expressions of disagreement and conflict

Once the issues have been defined, disagreement and conflict will often occur. This is natural and should be expected. Good negotiators never try to avoid this phase because they realise that this process of give and take is where successful deals are made.

Disagreement and conflict, handled properly, will eventually bring negotiators together. If handled poorly, they will widen the differences. Conflict has a way of bringing out different points of view, and crystallising the real wants and needs of the negotiators.

When presenting the issues, most negotiators will explain what they 'want'. It is the task of the other negotiator to find out what they 'need', or will settle for. Few negotiators will get all they want, even in a successful negotiation. But good negotiators will work to get as much as possible, yet understand compromise may be necessary, and a modification of goals may be required.

This confrontation can involve stress. It is important to remember, therefore, that conflict resolution under these circumstances is *not a test of power but an opportunity to reveal what people need*. Properly understood, this should lead to possible areas of agreement or compromise.

Hazel decides on the model she wants and asks the price. The salesperson says £250. Hazel is shocked because by her understanding of the ads it should be no more than £200 and she says so. The salesperson points out that this particular model has two features not included on the sale models. Hazel acknowledges this but still questions the additional cost.

Step 5. Reassessment and compromise

At some point, one party will normally move towards compromise. Statements reflecting this often begin with words like, 'Suppose that...?', 'What if...?', 'How would you feel about...?' When these statements begin, the other negotiator should listen carefully to see if an attempt to compromise is being offered. The response should be carefully stated. Too quick an attempt to pin something down may cause the other party to withdraw because the climate may not seem conducive to giving and getting.

When responding to offers it is a good practice to restate them. 'You will sell me this vehicle, as it is, for £300 less than the sticker price?' This response has at least three advantages:

1. The offer may be improved because the seller may get the impression that your echo is a negative.
2. The seller may attempt to justify the price. This will provide opportunities, for challenge.
3. An echo gives you time to think about a counter offer. Remember, however, that if the other negotiator echoes your offer, you simply confirm it, not sweeten it. Your confirmation forces the other negotiator to accept it, reject it, or suggest an alternative.

> After some discussion, Hazel says, 'I just can't pay that much. I'll look elsewhere.' The salesperson suggests a cheaper model but Hazel stands firm. The salesperson then says, 'Could you afford £220?' Hazel replies, '£220?' The salesperson adds, 'That includes delivery and connection.' Hazel answers, 'I can't exceed £200.'

Step 6. Agreement in principle or settlement

When agreement is reached, it will be necessary to affirm it. A decision about how the final settlement will be obtained is needed, especially if additional approval is required. This normally means placing the agreed terms in writing. If possible, this should be done while the parties are together so they can agree on the language. This will reduce the danger of a misunderstanding later.

Since agreement is the ultimate objectives of any negotiation, it is important to identify the level of authority of the party you are negotiating with at the outset. Some sellers, for example, will negotiate in order to identify *your* position, and then inform you they do not have the authority to accept your terms. They then go to some unseen person who will reject the tentative 'agreement' in an attempt to manoeuvre a better deal for the seller.

When you have the authority to make an agreement, always strive to negotiate with a person who has the same level of authority.

> The salesperson responds to Hazel's offer of £200 by saying, 'I just couldn't do that but I will let you have it for £215.' Hazel replies, 'Well, all right. If that includes delivery and installation you can take the order.'

Summary

Below is a brief summary of the six steps common to each negotiation. Keep these in mind before you engage in your next negotiation.

Step 1

I plan to get to know the party with whom I will be negotiating. My objective will be to keep initial interaction friendly, relaxed and businesslike.

Step 2

I expect to share my goals and objectives with the other party. At the same time I anticipate learning the goals and objectives of the other side. If possible, the atmosphere during this step will be one of cooperation and mutual trust.

Step 3

To start the process, specific issues will be raised. I plan to study all issues *before* the negotiations begin to identify where my advantages might lie insofar as splitting or combining issues is concerned. Once this has been done, the issues can be dealt with one by one.

Step 4

Once the issues have been defined it is essential to express areas of disagreement or conflict. Only when this has been done will it be possible to resolve the differences in a way that is acceptable to both parties.

Step 5

The key to any successful negotiation is when both parties reassess their positions and determine what level of compromise is acceptable. During this step I plan to remember the give-get principle covered on page 18.

Step 6

The final step is when both parties affirm any agreements that have been reached. I plan to ensure that there is no misunderstanding later by putting the agreements in writing (when applicable), and sending a copy to the other side. Mutual agreement is the ultimate objective of any negotiation.

Reading review

This is a good time to reflect on what you have read. Completing the exercise below will help to stimulate your thinking.

Complete each of the following statements with the most appropriate choice. Answers are given on page 29.

1. In negotiating, it is beneficial to:
   (a) take a little time to get to know the other party.
   (b) get down to serious business immediately.

2. Step 2 of a negotiation gives the parties:
   (a) a chance to challenge each other's position.
   (b) an opportunity to express objectives.

3. Compromising in a negotiation:
   (a) is a sign of weakness.
   (b) may be necessary to get what you need.

4. As issues are being clarified it sometimes:
   (a) appears that the differences are irreconcilable.
   (b) becomes apparent that some issues are closely tied to each other.

5. When conflict occurs in a negotiation, you should:
   (a) work towards its constructive solution.
   (b) go to a less controversial item.

6. When a negotiator says, 'What if I were to install...?':
   (a) the reassessment and compromise step has begun.
   (b) the negotiator is showing weakness.

7. It is a good idea to:
   (a) learn the authority of the person you are dealing with in advance.
   (b) assume the other person's level of authority is the same as yours.

8. The courage and confidence necessary to start a negotiation:
   (a) are inbred.
   (b) come with a willingness to learn skills and prepare.

CHAPTER 10
Planning and Preparing for Negotiation

When schemes are laid in advance, it is surprising how
often circumstances fit in with them.

Sir William Osler

Successful negotiation does not result from chance, it comes
from the skilful implementation of a well thought out plan.

If there is something you wish to acquire through negotiation, be prepared to take a few risks. Good preparation will
help you to keep risks manageable, and provide you with a
feeling of confidence.

Whether you are negotiating with your local nursery for a
few shrubs, with an international contractor for the construc-
tion of a new plant, or with your teenager for the use of the
family car, planning will usually make the difference between
a poor solution and one which is ideal.

1. Where to start planning

Start by thinking through your objectives.

● What do you want? What are you willing to give for it?

- What do you need? What are you willing to give for it?
- What is your timetable for giving and getting?

Once you have your objectives established, concentrate on the issues and categorise them as major or minor concerns. Do this not only for your issues, but also for those you anticipate the other party will identify as theirs. Also, don't neglect issues which are common to both parties.

Factors to consider in the analysis of the issues
1. Economic impact on the parties
2. Supply and demand
3. Past precedent and standard practices
4. Time constraints
5. Legal implications and considerations
6. Long- and short-term advantages and disadvantages.

2. Where to get information

Answers to most of the questions raised during your preparation are available through research. Often, all you need to know can be obtained by asking questions of others who have had similar experiences, or by doing research in readily available resources. These resources can include:

- Buyer's guides and other published product information.
- Magazine and newspaper articles.
- Instructional and educational books and/or pamphlets.
- Reports by government and industrial groups.
- Corporate annual reports.
- Electronic databases (often available in public libraries).
- Your network of business associates and friends.
- Publications and surveys by professional and community groups.

3. Develop a time perspective

After you are satisfied with your study of objectives and issues, and have gathered the information to support your position, decide how much time you have to devote to your effort. Estimate time factors for your opponent as well. Time is often a pressure point which can force concessions you would prefer not to make. The same is true of the other party. If you can make time relatively important, it is often possible to hold out for better terms because the other person is in a hurry to conclude the deal.

4. Identify sources of power

The relative power of the parties is another key factor to consider during your preparation. Power in this instance is not defined as the ability to force an action, but rather to influence an outcome by logic, validity, or legitimacy of a position. The following are some positive sources of power:

- *Persistence.* Do not concede or back off at the first sign of resistance. Give the other party time to think and consider alternatives. Then try again.
- *Competition.* There is always competition for what you have whether it is money, ideas or products. Never forget that you always have options.
- *Expertise.* Use what you have. You will receive more consideration from people who believe you have more knowledge, skill, or expertise than they do.
- *Legitimacy.* Give yourself and your position legitimacy by using supportive documentation. This often has great influence whether deserved or not.
- *Involvement.* Get everyone involved. Personal involvement will often cause those participating in a negotiation to work hard to ensure it doesn't fail.
- *Attitude.* Do not relieve your tension on the other negotiator. If you need time to reduce stress, take a break. Try to maintain a win/win attitude.

Every successful negotiator has a game plan. Did you have one during your last negotiation?

The advantages of planning

Those who do thorough preparation enter a negotiation confident that they can achieve their goals. They know they are ready, come what may. Rewards as a result of this planning are especially high during the reassessment and compromise phase of the negotiation. This is because the value of what we want, and what we are willing to give up, have been thoroughly considered. Possible points of concession have been identified, as well as those which we are not willing to yield. We can take whatever action is appropriate when the opportunity presents itself.

CHAPTER 11
Buying and Selling

Case study

Barney wants to buy a car. He spotted a good quality second-hand car on a dealer's lot at the weekend. He would buy it immediately if he had more cash. The dealer will only give him £1200 trade in for his present car. The car Barney wants is really good, and the chances are that it will be sold soon. Barney has planned carefully and decided he can swing the deal if he can sell his present vehicle to a private party for around £1500. This would give him £1350 for a down payment and £150 for accessories he wishes to add. The car is in good condition except for a couple of minor dents in the bumper. The roof rack for his present car won't fit the new one, but can probably be sold and that will help. His new stereo system (installed last month) can be removed and placed in the new car.

Millie, one of Barney's co-workers, heard that Barney wants to sell his car and plans to talk to him about it. Her daughter is graduating in three months' time and will need a car to drive to work. Millie can only afford about £1400 including any repairs that might be required and she needs to reserve some money to buy a roof rack. Her daughter has seen the car and thinks it's sporty, especially with the stereo. Millie checked the list price for the model of Barney's car, and knows the average wholesale price is £1200 and the average retail price is £1450.

Answer the following questions.

What are Barney's objectives?   What are Millie's objectives?

_____   _____

_____   _____

What are likely to be the points of conflict?

_____

What power does Barney have?   What power does Millie have?

_____   _____

What are some possible points of compromise?

_____

_____

Now turn to page 69 to check your thoughts with those of the author.

CHAPTER 12

High Expectations are Healthy

Your level of expectation has a direct relationship to what you achieve in a negotiation! Studies have verified that people with high expectations usually get more favourable agreements through negotiation than those without similar levels of expectation. Let's examine this using the previous case study as an example.

1. In negotiating, if you set a high goal you will normally do better than a person with low expectations.
If, in the case study you just examined, Millie offered Barney £1200, she might get the car for a lower price than if she had started at £1350. Her only risk is that Barney could get angry. If this happened she could always raise her offer a little. Suppose Millie initially offered Barney £1200, and Barney said no but he would accept £1450 if Millie paid cash within 24 hours. Barney has made a concession and shown a willingness to bargain. Millie should do the same. For the purposes of discussion let's say she raises her offer to £1250, but because Barney came down £50 is no reason Millie should go up by an equal or greater amount.

2. **Successful negotiators are usually able to make consistently smaller concessions than their opponents.**

After much bargaining, Barney lowered his price to £1400 and Millie raised her offer to £1300. At this point Barney suggests splitting the difference. Millie now has the option to hold firm, split the difference, or make a modest increase in her offer to £1325. This may be a tough choice for Millie. Offering £1325 is better than splitting the difference, but she might want to hold firm for the moment.

3. **Another important characteristic of successful negotiators is that they tend to be unpredictable as to how much they will concede.**

Barney has already made concessions and might be willing to make more. Millie will never know unless she tests his resolve.

CHAPTER 13

Why is Tony Earning More Than Joe?

Apply the principle

As in any sport, negotiating skills grow when they are practised using real-life situations. To start practising the principles just presented, identify the reasons Tony is earning more than Joe in the case below.

Case study

Joe and Tony are salesmen for the Reliance Rug Company. They are paid a standard commission based on the total of their individual sales. Both have the same level of authority to bargain with customers. They do have different attitudes towards bargaining, however, and their differences are often reflected in their incomes. Last year, for instance, they both sold identical amounts of comparable carpeting but Tony earned about £2500 more than Joe. See if you can identify why this occurred in the following summary of their respective negotiating practices.

Joe approaches customers as though price was their only consideration. He takes little time to discuss the virtues of the product, and in an effort to win the customers will often offer a discount before it even becomes an issue. Having set the stage for negotiating, he is anxious to close the deal quickly, and will make reductions in price in response to any hesitation by the buyer.

Tony makes a strong initial effort to sell the buyer the benefits of a carpet that will meet the buyer's needs. Tony does this because he feels this is of greater concern to the customer than price. Tony really expects to receive the normal retail price for what he sells, and very seldom volunteers a discount. If the customer raises the issue, Tony will negotiate to ensure a sale, but any concession he makes will be small and well earned by the buyer.

List as many reasons as you can why Tony is earning more than Joe. Check your answers with those of the author on page 70.

_____

_____

_____

CHAPTER 14
Strategies and Tactics

In the next few pages you will discover strategies and tactics to help you become an effective negotiator. Options are almost endless, and no attempt is made to cover all of them here. Those discussed are basic ploys which enjoy a good record of success.

These strategies and tactics are specialised tools you must know how to recognise, use, and defend against. They need to be learned and practised until they become an effective part of your negotiating activities.

Negotiators soon learn that to be successful you have to give in order to get. It's an essential fundamental. The skill is the ability to determine what to give, when to give, why to give, how much to give, and what to expect in return. To be an expert negotiator a person has to know how to manoeuvre so that what they *give* they can afford, and what they *get* will satisfy their needs. The techniques used to achieve this goal are referred to as strategies and tactics. *A strategy is the overall plan of action employed in a negotiation. Tactics are the step-by-step method used to implement the strategy.* Below are some strategies, and examples of how they can be applied.

Jane and Bill buy a house

Jane and Bill decided three months ago to buy a new home. Their first choice is a house in a new development, and priced at £55,000 (about £5000 above their limit). Jane thinks they should make an offer, but Bill doubts they could get the price down enough to make a difference.

Jane decided to do some research on the development anyway and learned that several of the houses, including the one they like, have been on the market almost a year. All are quality homes, but because of the state of the economy, sales have been slow. Jane convinces Bill they have nothing to lose by making an offer. After some careful planning they make an appointment to see the agent for the development.

Approach

Jane and Bill informed the agent that they really like the house and might be sincerely interested at a lower price, such as £45,000.

Strategy

LOWBALL. They are going for the lowest possible price and are trying to buy at what they estimate the builder's cost to be.

The agent sounded shocked and said, 'That's impossible, the developer wouldn't even consider it!' Jane and Bill anticipated this response, and asked 'If you won't accept £45,000, what will you take?'

PINPOINT THE NEED. It has been established that the seller will take less than the asking price but not £45,000. The task now is to pinpoint how much less than £55,000.

Approach

The agent did some calculations before he said '£50,000 but you need at least £10,000 cash down.' Jane and Bill had hoped for a lower counter offer, but were prepared for the £50,000 response. Bill tried another strategy by saying, 'The down payment is no problem, but I understand the house next door sold for £8,000 less than the asking price. Why won't you do the same for us?'

The agent reacted by saying, 'That was a more expensive house, and we had more latitude. Perhaps the builder could trim the price a bit more, say to £49,000, if you could give us your offer in writing today, along with the £10,000 deposit.' Jane and Bill, sensing they were getting close to their goal, replied, 'We really do like this house, but it is still more than we want to pay. Please excuse us while we discuss ways in which we might increase our offer. Would you please reassess your position too?'

Strategy

CHALLENGE. A strategy designed to put the other party on the defensive in an effort to win some concessions. Added here to PINPOINTING to assist in determining what the seller will actually take.

DEFER. Jane and Bill take a break to allow themselves and the agent time to reassess their positions. Deferring a decision to make this possible often proves that patience pays.

Approach

Bill and Jane returned in an hour and offered £47,000. The agent told them: 'I phoned the builder while you were away to see if further concessions were possible. He gave a little, but £47,000 just won't do. However, if you would be willing to split the difference and make it £48,000, we can make a deal, provided you sign the papers and put down your £10,000 today.' Jane and Bill looked at each other and accepted with pleasure.

Strategy

SPLIT THE DIFFERENCE. Jane and Bill carefully calculated their counter offer in hope that the seller would either accept the offer or suggest SPLITTING THE DIFFERENCE.

The result was a sales price at the midpoint between the seller's last offer and Jane and Bill's counter proposal.

Now that you have had the opportunity to examine some strategies and see them at work in a sample negotiation, it's time to learn others.

These are also strategies where both parties can win. In addition, they are strategies that can move you from the minor to the major leagues.

The best way to learn these strategies is to apply them. Tick the box if the strategy described will fit into your negotiating style.

Salami ☐

Salami is a technique used to achieve an objective a little bit at a time rather than in one giant step. This strategy is said to have been named by Mátyás Rákosis, General Secretary of the Hungarian Communist Party, who explained it in this way:

When you want to get hold of a salami which your opponents are strenuously defending, you must not grab at it. You must start by carving yourself a very thin slice. The owner of the salami will hardly notice it, or at least he will not mind very much. The next day you will carve another slice, then still another. And so, little by little, the salami will pass into your possession.

> You want to buy five acres of land from an elderly gentleman, who for sentimental reasons does not want to sell more than one acre now. You are in no hurry to acquire all five. How would you approach the old gentleman?
>
> Check your response with the one below.

Fait accompli ☐

Residents of a community called Hillview woke up one morning to discover a local developer removing the top of a peak, which was an appealing part of their view. The developer did not have a permit, but once removed the hill top could not be restored. The strategy he used is called *fait accompli*. He took action to accomplish his objective, risking acceptance because he did not wish to spend the necessary time, effort or expense in following the established guidelines. In effect, the developer said, 'I did what I wanted to, so now what are you going to do?' This can be risky. Those who employ it must understand and accept the consequences if the strategy fails. For example, the same developer later put up a fence in violation of boundary regulations. This time the local people protested and he was required to tear down the fence and move it to a legal boundary at considerable expense.

Answer: Applying the salami strategy
Offer to buy one acre now with an option to buy the other four, one acre at a time, over the next four years.

Some examples of *fait accompli* are given below. Indicate how you would respond to them.

Fait accompli	Response
A contract was sent to you containing a provision you did not agree to and find unacceptable.	
You took your old vehicle to a garage to obtain an estimate for repairs. When you returned you found the garage had already repaired it and presented you with a bill for £300.	

Possible responses to fait accompli
1. Use *fait accompli* yourself. Delete the unacceptable clauses from the contract and send it back.
2. Several options, including the following, are possible:
   - Refuse payment.
   - Appeal to higher authority. Take it to the owner.
   - Call in a lawyer, or threaten to sue. If by-laws or local regulations have been violated, appeal to the town hall for assistance.
   - Tell others what happened to you. Document your case and let the public and others in business know of the unethical practices.

Standard practice   ☐

This is a strategy used to convince others to do or not to do something because of so-called 'standard practices'. It often works very well because it infers it is the best way to do whatever needs to be done, and is probably a safe approach.

Standard contracts are an example of this strategy. The party suggesting a standard contract assumes no one would want to change it, because it reflects what others routinely agree to under the circumstances. Often the other party will accept this as a fact of life: however, those who wish to test it can have good results.

A plumber who was contracted to install plumbing in a new home told his customer that the payment terms were 30 per cent when he started the job, 60 per cent when it was half completed and 10 per cent on completion. When the customer refused to accept the agreement, the contractor said the terms were industry standards and showed him the standard contract to prove it. The customer refused to sign. Finally the contractor agreed to 30 per cent at the start, 30 per cent at the half-way point and 40 per cent upon completion. This assured the customer that the plumbing would be finished before the contractor could take his profit, but provided adequate funds for the plumber to carry out the project.

Deadlines

Time is critical to people and organisations. Consequently, deadlines can be an effective negotiation strategy. All too often we are aware of time pressures upon ourselves, but assume the other party has plenty of time. A better assumption would be that if we have deadlines, the other party probably has them too. The more we learn about the other party's deadlines, the better we can plan our strategies. When others attempt to force us to their deadlines, we should not hesitate to test them. Most sales in retail stores that 'start' on Tuesday and 'end' on Friday, can be negotiated so a buyer can take advantage of them on a Monday or Saturday as well. Many hotels will extend their check-out time beyond 12 noon if you are willing to negotiate for a later time. Proposals requested by the first of the month are often just as acceptable on the second. Deadlines are usually as demanding as we are willing to think they are. The more we know about the person or organisation that set them, the better we can evaluate what they really mean.

Before entering a negotiation, ask yourself these questions:

1. What actual deadlines and time constraints am I under? Are these self-imposed or controlled by someone else?
2. Are these deadlines realistic? Can I change them?
3. What deadlines might be controlling the other side? Can I use these to my advantage?

Here is a dialogue between Dick Thomas, a purchasing agent, and Rick Forest, an office equipment sales manager:

Mr Thomas: The word processors you are suggesting will meet our requirements. Can you provide three by next Monday for £1500?

Mr Forest: I am not sure we can. Because you also want the high speed printer, that puts the price for three over £2000.

Mr Thomas: That's more than our budget allows for this purchase.

Mr Forest: Well, I'm sorry about that. To meet your price, I would have to talk to my district manager and he is hard to reach.

What might Mr Thomas say to get Mr Forest to agree to supply the word processors for £1500, or at least make some price concession, with minimum delay?

_____

_____

When you have completed your response, compare it with the possibilities suggested at the bottom of page 49.

Feinting   ☐

Feinting gives the impression that one thing is desired when the primary objective is really something else. An employee, for example, may negotiate with the boss for a promotion when the real objective is a good increase in salary. If the promotion is forthcoming, so is the rise. If the promotion is not possible, a nice rise may be the consolation prize. Politicians use a variation of this strategy to test receptivity by the public to something they plan to do. Their planned action is 'leaked' by a 'reliable source' to test acceptability before a final decision is made. The public's response is then evaluated. If there is little opposition it is probably safe to proceed. If there is an adverse reaction, another approach can be explored.

Apparent withdrawal

Apparent withdrawal may include some deception as well as deferring and feinting. It attempts to make the other negotiator believe you have withdrawn from consideration of an issue when you really have not. Its purpose may be ultimately to get a concession or change in position. For example, the prospective buyer of a painting finds the seller unwilling to meet the price the buyer is prepared to pay. The buyer might say, 'I'm sorry but I can't meet your price. You know my price, so unless there is some movement on your part we can't do business.' The buyer then leaves. If the buyer has made a realistic offer, the seller may decide to make a concession. If not, the buyer can always go back with a slightly higher offer. In the meantime, of course, the buyer can consider other options.

Possible responses by Mr Thomas

'Well, I'm sorry we can't make a deal. I have an appointment this afternoon with High Speed and Quickline. Both have indicated they can provide comparable equipment at a cost within our budget. The department head who wants these machines is leaving for two weeks holiday tomorrow. He will make his choice before he leaves today.'

Good guy/Bad guy

The good guy/bad guy ploy is an internationally used strategy. One member of a negotiating team takes a hard-line approach while another member is friendly and easy to deal with. When the bad guy steps out for a few minutes, the good guy offers a deal that, under the circumstances, may seem too good to refuse. There are many versions of 'bad guys'. They may be solicitors, spouses, personnel representatives, accountants, sales managers, or economists.

One danger of using this strategy is that it will be recognised for what it is. Here are some ways to deal with it if you feel it is being used on you:

- Walk out.
- Use your own 'bad' guy.
- Tell them to drop the act and get down to business.

Limited authority

Limited authority is an attempt to force acceptance of a position by claiming anything else would require higher approval. Individuals who claim to have limited authority are difficult to negotiate with, because the reason they use not to meet your demands involves someone else, or some policy or practice over which they have no control. A salesperson who cannot give more than a 5 per cent cash discount, influence the delivery date, or accept a trade-in will not make concessions in those areas. Some negotiators will concede under these circumstances, while others will insist their offer be taken wherever necessary for approval or rejection. There is some risk that this will terminate the negotiation, but it does give the other party a chance to reassess their position gracefully.

Can you recognise and define the following?

	Yes	No
Salami	☐	☐
Fait accompli	☐	☐
Standard practice	☐	☐
Deadlines	☐	☐
Feinting	☐	☐
Apparent withdrawal	☐	☐
Good guy/Bad guy	☐	☐
Limited authority	☐	☐

CHAPTER 15
Eight Critical Mistakes

Now that we have considered some helpful strategies, let's think about some critical mistakes negotiators sometimes make. You must make every effort to avoid them!

Tick those you intend to avoid:

1. *Inadequate preparation* ☐
   Preparation provides a good picture of your options and allows for planned flexibility at the crunch points.

2. *Ignoring the give/get principle* ☐
   Each party needs to conclude the negotiation feeling something has been gained.

3. *Use of intimidating behaviour* ☐
   Research shows the tougher the tactics, the tougher the resistance. Persuasiveness, not dominance, makes for a more effective outcome.

4. *Impatience* ☐
   Give ideas and proposals time to work. Don't rush things; patience pays.

5. *Loss of temper* ☐
   Strong negative emotions are a deterrent to
   developing a cooperative environment and creating
   solutions.

6. *Talking too much and listening too little* ☐
   If you love to listen, you will gain knowledge,
   and if you incline your ear, you will become wise.
   Sirach

7. *Arguing instead of influencing* ☐
   Your position can be best explained by education,
   not stubbornness.

8. *Ignoring conflict* ☐
   Conflict is the substance of negotiation. Learn to
   accept and resolve it, not avoid it.

CHAPTER 16

Acceptance Time and Post-negotiation Review

Two additional important considerations for the negotiator are acceptance time and the post-negotiation review. They are explained below.

Acceptance time

As you go through the negotiating process, be ever mindful of the need for acceptance time. *People need time to accept anything new or different.* Parties enter negotiations hoping to get what they want quickly and easily. This is not always possible. Sometimes they have made incorrect assumptions or perhaps have some misconceptions. The high price desired by the seller, or the low price hoped for by the buyer is not as easily obtained as they had anticipated. Readjustments are needed. These take time. Wishes become reality only through hard bargaining, readjustment and compromise.

Post-negotiation review

Do an analysis following each negotiation. This will help you to identify reasons for your success or failure, and will be valuable information in future negotiations. Examine the strengths and weaknesses of your opponent's approach as well as your own, and file them away for reference prior to your next negotiation.

The *Negotiator's Guide to Preparation* presented in Chapter 17 is an excellent reference to guide your post-negotiation review.

CHAPTER 17

Negotiator's Guide to Preparation

Use this chapter both for preparation and for your post-negotiation review. It won't take long for a minor negotiation, and you can't afford to miss anything in a major one.

Checklist

1. **Define goals and objectives** ☐
   - Exactly what do I want from this negotiation?
   - What do I have to get to meet my needs?
   - What am I willing to give up to get what I want?
   - What are my time and economic requirements for this negotiation?

2. **Clarify the issues** ☐
   - What are the issues as I see them?
   - What is the supporting framework for my position?
   - How will I present it to the other party?
   - What are the issues as seen by the other party?
   - How will they support their position?
   - What appear to be the significant differences in the way the parties view the issues?

3. **Gather information** ☐
   - Who will I be negotiating with and what do I know about them? How do they approach a negotiation? What are their ego needs?
   - When and where will the negotiation take place? What advantages or disadvantages do the alternatives have for me? ... for the other party?
   - What are the economic, political and human implications of the issues?
   - What personal power do I have that can be used constructively in this negotiation?

4. **Humanise and set the climate** ☐
   - How can I best establish rapport with the other party?
   - How can I establish a win/win climate?

5. **Prepare for conflict** ☐
   - What will be the major points of conflict?
   - How will I determine what the other party needs as compared with what they want?

6. **Compromise/resolution of the issues** ☐
   - How will I attempt to resolve conflict? How will I respond to the other party's attempt to resolve conflict?
   - What concessions am I prepared to make? Under what conditions?
   - What do I expect in return for my concessions?

7. **Agreement and confirmation** ☐
   - How formal must it be?
   - What approval process will be required? How long will it take?
   - What implementation steps will be needed?

CHAPTER 18
Measure Your Progress

It is time now to review the progress you have made. The following 20 statements are either true or false. Each correct answer is worth 5 points. If your score is 80 or better you have the knowledge necessary to become an excellent negotiator. If your score is below 80, reread this book and retake the test. Remember, good negotiators are 'made not born'.

Reading review

For each statement below, put a tick under True or False.

True *False*

_____ _____ 1. Negotiating skills can be learned but they require consistent practice.

_____ _____ 2. Good negotiators are willing to research and analyse issues carefully.

_____ _____ 3. Negotiating is one area in which patience is not a virtue.

_____ _____ 4. Advance planning is not possible in negotiating.

_____ _____ 5. Successful negotiators stress winning at any cost.

True False

_____ _____ 6. Too much advance preparation reduces your flexibility.

_____ _____ 7. Compromise is a tool used by weak negotiators to save face.

_____ _____ 8. Conflict is an important part of any negotiation.

_____ _____ 9. People need to be given time to accept changes and new ideas.

_____ _____ 10. Always do a post-negotiation analysis to improve your learning experience.

_____ _____ 11. Most of the information we need prior to a negotiation can be obtained by asking questions and doing some basic research.

_____ _____ 12. When negotiating, the more authority you have the better.

_____ _____ 13. Your objectives for every negotiation should be well thought out.

_____ _____ 14. Negotiators should be well versed in the techniques of conflict resolution.

_____ _____ 15. Your expectation level has a direct relationship to what you achieve in a negotiation.

_____ _____ 16. Any time we attempt to influence another person through an exchange of ideas, or something of material value, we are negotiating.

_____ _____ 17. It is possible for both parties to win in a negotiation because everyone has different needs and values.

_____ _____ 18. You must give to get is a basic rule of negotiating.

_____ _____ 19. Competition for what you have whether it is money, ideas or products, is a source of power.

____ ____ 20. *Successful Negotiation* is a great start to acquiring negotiating skills but it should be followed by additional reading, training and practice.

TOTAL CORRECT_____ (ANSWERS ON PAGE 63)

CHAPTER 19

Answers to Review Questions

Check your answers to the review questions. If you missed any, it will be helpful to review the sections of the book in which they were covered.

1. True   Practice makes perfect.
2. True   An essential effort.
3. False Patience and fortitude are essential.
4. False Planning is one of the secrets of success.
5. False Successful negotiators believe it is a win/win process.
6. False Advance preparation enables flexibility.
7. False Compromise is a basic method of conflict resolution.
8. True   When there is no disagreement, there is no need to negotiate.
9. True   Acceptance time should be an integral part of the plan.
10. True Learn from experience.
11. True
12. False Too much authority can lead to a settlement before all the options have been tested.

13. True   Your must know what you want to achieve.
14. True
15. True   Those who expect little achieve little.
16. True   This is an ideal result of negotiation.
17. True
18. True
19. True   An especially great power source when linked with patience.
20. True   Review it prior to any negotiation.

Make plans now to apply what you have learned!

Reflect for moment on what you have been learning – then develop a personal action plan using the following guide to apply what you have learned.

Think over the material you have read, the self-analysis questionnaires, the case studies and the reinforcement exercises. What did you learn about negotiating? What did you learn about yourself? How can you apply what you have learned to your personal life? Your business life? Your community life? Make a commitment to become a better negotiator. Design a personal action plan that will help you to accomplish this goal.

CHAPTER 20
A Personal Action Plan

_____
Name and Date

1. My current negotiating skills are effective in the following areas:

   _____

   _____

   _____

2. I need to improve my negotiating skills in the following areas:

   _____

   _____

   _____

3. My negotiating skills improvement goals are as follows: (Be sure your goals are specific, attainable and measurable.)

   _____

   _____

   _____

4. These people and resources can help me to accomplish my goals:

   _____

   _____

   _____

5. These are my action steps and timetable to accomplish my goals:

   _____

   _____

   _____

Voluntary contract

Sometimes our desire to improve personal skills can be assisted by making a contract with a friend, spouse, or supervisor. If you believe a contract would help you, use the form on the following page. If the contract provided doesn't suit you, negotiate one that does.

VOLUNTARY
CONTRACT*

I, _____, hereby

(Your name)

agree to meet with the individual designated below within thirty days to discuss my progress toward incorporating the techniques and ideas of negotiation presented in this programme. The purpose of this meeting will be to review areas of strength and establish action steps for areas where improvement may still be required.

_____

Signature

I agree to meet the above person on

_____

Month   *Date*   *Time*

at the following location.

_____

_____

Signature

*This agreement can be initiated either by you or your superior. Its purpose is to motivate you to incorporate concepts and techniques of this programme into your daily activities. It also provides a degree of accountability between you and a person you respect.

CHAPTER 21

Author's Answers to the Case Studies

Buying and selling (page 36)

Barney's objective is to sell his existing vehicle for enough to finance a new one. He wants £1500 but he knows the dealer will only offer him £1200. He needs £1350 to finance the new one. The chances are good that he will be satisfied with £1350.

Millie's objective is to buy a good used car for her daughter for under £1400. She wants to keep a small reserve for repairs and enough to buy a roof rack.

Points of conflict between Barney and Millie are likely to be price and equipment to be included with the car. Barney's power comes from having a car in good repair, that Millie's daughter likes, in Millie's price range. Additional power comes from the fact that Barney's car will also be attractive to others.

Millie has power because there are many used cars in her price range to choose from. Millie also has power because time is important to Barney, and Millie has three months to look around.

Possible points of compromise include the price, whether or not the roof rack and/or stereo are included, and what can be done about the minor dents.

Many variations are possible and both parties should think them through before negotiations begin.

Why is Tony earning more than Joe? (page 40)

Tony sells the customer on the product first by showing how it will fulfil the customer's needs. Once the buyer has this assurance, price may become less important. If the buyer selects another product or vendor, some need satisfaction might have to be risked. If Tony does not suggest a discount, many buyers will pay the retail price. He always has price flexibility to fall back on. Consequently, Tony's high expectations pay off. Tony makes the buyer work for concessions. These cost Tony little but make buyers feel good when they win one. Tony earns more because he sells at least as much as Joe and at a consistently higher price.

APPENDIX A

Managing Conflict During Negotiation

The term 'negotiation' itself suggests the presence of conflict. It may be minor or a monumental block in achieving success for the parties involved. The parties may mean well, but each is trying to achieve what they perceive to be the best objective. Conflict is present because of:

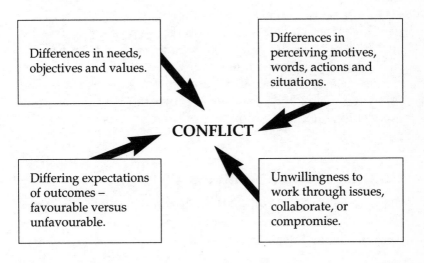

Differences in needs, objectives and values.

Differences in perceiving motives, words, actions and situations.

CONFLICT

Differing expectations of outcomes – favourable versus unfavourable.

Unwillingness to work through issues, collaborate, or compromise.

Conflict becomes unhealthy when it is avoided or approached on a win/lose basis. Animosities will develop, communications will break down, trust and mutual support will deteriorate, and hostilities will result. The damage is usually difficult (sometimes impossible) to repair.

Conflict is healthy when it causes the negotiators to explore new ideas, test their position and beliefs, and stretch their imagination. When conflict is dealt with constructively, the negotiators may be stimulated to greater creativity, which should lead to a wider variety of alternatives and better results.

Negotiators do not always get all they 'want', even in a successful negotiation. But they do work hard to get what they need. Each negotiator wants to get as much as she/he can, yet each knows a compromise may be necessary, that original goals may have to be altered.

If a negotiator is to get what she/he wants, the other party must understand her/his point of view. This requires that the substance from which negotiating positions were developed be made clear. This is a process of education, not argumentation.

Good negotiators always look for ways to convert divergent ideas into channels of common interest. They emphasise and build on matters that can be agreed upon and avoid dwelling on points of difference.

Five basic styles of conflict resolution are described on the following page. It is easy to identify those that have the highest likelihood of producing positive results in a negotiation.

Conflict resolution styles

There are five basic approaches to conflict resolution. They can be summarised as follows. Indicate the one you are most likely to use in a negotiation.

Style	Characteristic Behaviour	User Justification
Avoidance ☐	Non-confrontational. Ignores or passes over issues. Denies issues are a problem.	Differences too minor or too great to resolve. Attempts might damage relationships or create even greater problems.
Accommodating ☐	Agreeable, non-assertive behaviour. Cooperative even at the expense of personal goals.	Not worth risking damage to relationships or general disharmony.
Win/Lose ☐	Confrontational, assertive and aggressive. Must win at any cost.	Survival of the fittest. Must prove superiority. Most ethically or professionally correct.
Compromising ☐	Important all parties achieve basic goals and maintain good relationships. Aggressive but cooperative.	No one person or idea is perfect. There is more than one good way to do anything. You must give to get.
Problem Solving ☐	Needs of both parties are legitimate and important. High respect for mutual support. Assertive and cooperative.	When parties will openly discuss issues, a mutually beneficial solution can be found without anyone making a major concession.

COMPROMISING AND PROBLEM SOLVING STYLES PROVIDE THE STRONGEST BASIS FOR WIN/WIN OUTCOMES.

Appendix A

You may find the following diagram helpful in understanding conflict resolution styles.

Answer the following questions:

1. Which style is the most uncooperative and least assertive?
   _____

2. Which style is characterised by assertive behaviour, yet represents the maximum in cooperation? _____

3. Which style is totally cooperative but unassertive? _____

4. Which style is totally assertive and uncooperative? _____

5. Which style takes the middle ground on assertiveness and cooperation? _____

APPENDIX B

Negotiating a Starting Salary – An Example of the Practical Application of Negotiating Principles

Jackie Stevens has been unemployed for about three months. She was a middle management level Director of Operations in a technical manufacturing firm. She has a well thought out job objective in mind and has worked hard on her job search. During the last two weeks she has had multiple interviews with three different companies. Two have already made her offers at an acceptable level. The third company with the position she really wants has indicated they plan to extend her an offer within the current week. She has carefully discussed her offers from the other two companies with them and has been successful in getting them to hold their offers open for a few days so she can evaluate them fully. Her task now is to decide how she will approach the new offer when it is extended.

Jackie realises that she must first think through some basics. These include:

● Does the position meet her career criteria at this point in her professional life?

- Does she understand the company culture and believe she will be comfortable in that environment?
- Does she fully understand the duties and responsibilities of the position and want to undertake them?
- Is she prepared to accept the position enthusiastically if her negotiations are successful?

If she has not already done so, it is also time for Jackie to do some intense research to build her knowledge of all three companies. Her research will provide answers to some of the above questions and provide her with objective information for comparison purposes. Her research should include the following elements:

- Does the size of the company and its sales volume indicate it is stable and competitive in the current economy?
- Is the company financially sound and profitable?
- Are the company's products and services state of the art?
- Is the company vulnerable because of outdated manufacturing practices or new products and services under development by competitors?
- Is there a strategic planning process in place?
- Is the company publicly or privately held?
- Does the company appear to have a management style compatible with your own?
- What does the company's history reflect in terms of mergers, acquisitions, reorganisations and downsizing?
- Is the company known for sound business practices and ethical relationships with its competitors, customers and employees?
- Does the climate for personal achievement and growth appear to be present for those who earn it?

Hopefully, Jackie has already developed a list of the key elements she wants in a compensation package. This is easily accomplished by preparing a list of those items that are sometimes included as part of compensation. These items can then be ranked in order of importance and some thought given to the dimensions of the various aspects of the desired package. Once this has been done Jackie should review the data from the standpoint of what she wants versus what she needs. What she wants will most likely include (and justifiably so) some elements of fantasy about her worth. What she needs is what she has to have to meet her basic survival needs. Somewhere between the two, is the package which she will recognise as reasonable, and accept. One way to approach this determination is as follows:

TARGET COMPENSATION WORKSHEET						
Compensation Factors	RANKING	LAST POSITION	WANT	NEED	ACCEPT	OFFER
Base Salary						
Benefits Basic Health						
Major Medical						
Life Insurance						
Retirement						
Holidays						
Disability						
Bonus/Incentives						
Signing Bonus						
Stock Options						
Deferred Comp						
Moving Expenses						
Temporary Living Expenses						

Some positions (usually at the more senior levels) offer certain perks. If Jackie feels these are possible at her level, she should make a list of those she feels are important to the performance of her job and negotiate accordingly. These might include:

Possible perks

- Car Allowance
- Car Phone
- Expense Account
- Club Memberships
- VIP Travel
- PC/Fax at Home
- Credit Cards
- Financial Planning
- Tax Assistance
- Low Interest Mortgage Loans

As soon as Jackie has completed her research and outlined what she wants and what she needs, she should make an effort to check them against an objective analysis of the job market. She can do this in several ways including the following:

- What do current employees earn?
  This can sometimes be obtained from the interviewer, from employees or through the use of networking with friends and associates in the same industry.
- What do similar positions in the industry pay?
  This information is often available from industry and professional salary surveys as well as networking.
- What regional factors may apply?
  Salaries paid for the same type of work in different geographic areas may vary due to economic conditions, cost of living and the law of supply and demand. Professional and industrial surveys often note these differences. Chambers of Commerce may also be able to help sort this out.

- What is the current impact of the law of supply and demand?
  Local and national news are often good sources of this type of information as are surveys, Chambers of Commerce, the Department of Education and Employment, and local unemployment agencies.
- Is the company in transition, causing its salary levels to be slightly inflated to attract new people, or slightly deflated because they are recovering from hard times?
  Answers to this question may be difficult to obtain but a little research in appropriate business journals and newspapers may be an excellent source of this type of information.

Now that Jackie has examined her own goals, needs, wants and the supporting substance for each, she should begin to consider what the company's issues may be and how they might affect her own negotiating strategy.

Issues from the company's perspective

- Does the applicant fully meet or exceed job requirements?
  Jackie will need to be prepared to demonstrate how well her qualifications match the job requirements and the extent of the contributions she will be able to make in the first few months of her employment.
- Will the candidate be able to adapt to the company culture and perform up to the level her qualifications suggest?
- Is the personal chemistry right for the development of effective relationships?
- Can she be offered an attractive salary package that will be compatible with the company structure?
- Does she have the long-term potential required to meet the company's needs?
- Is she likely to stay long enough to return their investment in hiring and training costs?

If the answers to the foregoing questions are yes, the climate for negotiations should be very positive. If the answer to any of them could be no, or maybe, Jackie needs to plan how she will respond.

Identify sources of power

The relative power of the parties is another key factor to consider during preparation. Power in this instance is not defined as the ability to force an action, but rather to influence an outcome by logic, validity, or legitimacy of a position. Jackie already has several points of power working in her favour.

- She has two offers already which should give her confidence as she enters the current negotiation for which she is preparing. Her power will increase again when the third company makes its offer. She must use this power carefully but it arises from the fact that once a prospective employer has made their first choice they do not like to go back to another candidate or reinstitute the search. Consequently, they will make every reasonable effort to meet Jackie's requirements.
- The fact that Jackie already has two offers demonstrates that there is always competition for what you have, whether it is money, ideas or products. Negotiators must never forget they have options.
- Jackie obviously has considerable expertise and has convinced her interviewers accordingly. She will need to be prepared to reinforce that if the negotiations become difficult. Employers are not inclined to improve an offer just because the applicant needs the money. They may improve it, however, if they are presented with substantive reasons.

At this point, Jackie has defined her goals and objectives, gathered information to assure herself this is a position she really wants, determined what she needs vs. what she wants, decided what she will accept, tested it against market-place data, and considered what some of the company's issues may be.

Now she needs to think about how she will continue to build the rapport she has already established within the company and how she will express her desire for a win/win outcome if negotiations are necessary. She will carefully review any concessions she is willing to make and what she expects in return. This may require some application of the principles of conflict resolution and she will practise a constructive approach.

Finally, she will give some thought to when she will accept the offer if it is acceptable. She may wish to accept it on the spot or perhaps will ask the employer to hold the position for her for a few days so she can sort it out. At this point, she may well want to go back to her other two offers for further negotiation.

She should, of course, ask for the final offer in writing.

Further Reading from Kogan Page

Assert Yourself: How to Do a Good Deal Better with Others, Robert Sharpe

How To Be A Better Negotiator, John Mattock and Jons Ehrenborg

Succeed For Yourself, Richard Denny

Better Management Skills

Creative Decision-making, H B Gelatt

Develop Your Assertiveness, Sue Bishop

Empowering People, Jane Smith

How to Motivate People, Twyla Dell

Leadership Skills for Women, M Manning and P Haddock

Team Building, Robert B Maddux